EMMANUEL JOSEPH

Synergy in Diversity, Elevating Business Through Multicultural Leadership and Global Innovation

Copyright © 2025 by Emmanuel Joseph

All rights reserved. No part of this publication may be reproduced, stored or transmitted in any form or by any means, electronic, mechanical, photocopying, recording, scanning, or otherwise without written permission from the publisher. It is illegal to copy this book, post it to a website, or distribute it by any other means without permission.

First edition

This book was professionally typeset on Reedsy.
Find out more at reedsy.com

Contents

1	Chapter 1: The Power of Diversity in Modern Business	1
2	Chapter 2: Building a Multicultural Leadership Team	3
3	Chapter 3: Fostering Inclusive Work Environments	5
4	Chapter 4: Leveraging Global Innovation	6
5	Chapter 5: Embracing Cultural Intelligence	7
6	Chapter 6: Strategies for Multicultural Team Collaboration	8
7	Chapter 7: Overcoming Challenges in Diverse Workplaces	9
8	Chapter 8: The Role of Technology in Promoting Diversity	10
9	Chapter 9: The Impact of Diversity on Employee Engagement	11
10	Chapter 10: Global Trends in Diversity and Inclusion	12
11	Chapter 11: Measuring the Impact of Diversity Initiatives	13
12	Chapter 12: The Future of Work: Embracing Diversity and...	14
13	Chapter 13: Case Studies of Successful Multicultural...	15
14	Chapter 14: The Role of Education and Training in Diversity...	16
15	Chapter 15: Leadership for a Diverse and Innovative Future	17

1

Chapter 1: The Power of Diversity in Modern Business

The Evolution of Diversity in the Workplace Over the years, the concept of diversity has transitioned from mere compliance to a critical business strategy. Initially, diversity efforts focused on affirmative action and anti-discrimination policies. However, the contemporary workplace recognizes that embracing diversity goes beyond these basic principles. It is now seen as a means to drive innovation, enhance employee engagement, and improve organizational performance.

The Business Case for Diversity Companies that actively promote diversity and inclusion often see tangible benefits. A diverse workforce brings together varied perspectives, which can lead to more innovative problem-solving and decision-making. Research indicates that organizations with diverse leadership teams are more likely to outperform their less diverse counterparts financially. This chapter examines real-world examples of how diversity contributes to business success.

Understanding the Dimensions of Diversity Diversity encompasses a wide range of characteristics, including but not limited to, race, gender, age, sexual orientation, cultural background, and more. It's crucial for businesses to understand these dimensions to foster an inclusive environment. This section explores the different facets of diversity and how each aspect can contribute to a richer workplace culture.

The Role of Leadership in Promoting Diversity Effective leadership is key to creating and sustaining a diverse workplace. Leaders must not only champion diversity initiatives but also model inclusive behavior. This chapter discusses how leaders can inspire their teams to embrace diversity and how they can implement policies that promote a culture of inclusion.

2

Chapter 2: Building a Multicultural Leadership Team

Identifying Potential Leaders from Diverse Backgrounds Building a multicultural leadership team starts with recognizing talent from various backgrounds. Organizations should actively seek out and nurture potential leaders from diverse groups. This chapter offers strategies for identifying and supporting individuals who can bring unique perspectives and skills to leadership roles.

Developing Inclusive Leadership Skills Inclusive leadership goes beyond traditional management skills. It involves empathy, cultural competence, and the ability to create an environment where all team members feel valued. This chapter explores the essential skills needed for inclusive leadership and provides practical tips for developing these abilities.

Overcoming Bias in Leadership Selection Unconscious bias can hinder the development of a truly diverse leadership team. Organizations must implement measures to identify and mitigate bias in their leadership selection processes. This section discusses various methods for reducing bias and ensuring fair opportunities for all candidates.

The Impact of Multicultural Leadership on Business Outcomes Multicultural leadership can drive better business outcomes by fostering innovation and improving decision-making processes. This chapter presents case studies and research findings that demonstrate the positive impact of diverse leadership teams on organizational performance.

3

Chapter 3: Fostering Inclusive Work Environments

Creating a Culture of Inclusion An inclusive workplace culture is one where all employees feel respected, valued, and empowered. This chapter explores the elements of an inclusive culture and provides practical steps for fostering such an environment within an organization.

Implementing Diversity Training Programs Diversity training programs are essential for educating employees about the importance of inclusion and how to practice it in their daily work. This section discusses different types of diversity training and how to implement them effectively.

Addressing Microaggressions and Discrimination Microaggressions and discrimination can undermine efforts to create an inclusive workplace. Organizations must take proactive steps to address these issues. This chapter offers strategies for recognizing and responding to microaggressions and discriminatory behaviors.

Promoting Work-Life Balance and Flexibility Inclusive workplaces recognize the importance of work-life balance and offer flexible work arrangements to accommodate diverse needs. This section examines how organizations can implement policies that promote work-life balance and support employees' well-being.

4

Chapter 4: Leveraging Global Innovation

The Global Landscape of Innovation Innovation is no longer confined to specific regions or industries. In today's interconnected world, groundbreaking ideas can emerge from anywhere. This chapter provides an overview of the global innovation landscape and highlights key trends shaping the future.

Collaborating Across Borders Cross-border collaboration can lead to significant breakthroughs by combining diverse perspectives and expertise. This chapter explores the benefits and challenges of international collaboration and offers strategies for successful cross-border partnerships.

Harnessing Technology for Global Innovation Technology plays a crucial role in enabling global innovation. From communication tools to data analytics, technology can facilitate collaboration and drive creative solutions. This section discusses the technological advancements that support global innovation efforts.

Case Studies of Global Innovation Success Real-world examples of successful global innovation can provide valuable insights and inspiration. This chapter presents case studies of organizations that have effectively leveraged diversity and multicultural leadership to achieve remarkable innovations.

5

Chapter 5: Embracing Cultural Intelligence

Understanding Cultural Intelligence (CQ) Cultural intelligence (CQ) is the ability to navigate and adapt to different cultural contexts. This chapter introduces the concept of CQ and explains its importance in today's diverse business environment.

Developing Cultural Awareness Developing cultural awareness involves recognizing and appreciating cultural differences. This section offers practical tips for increasing cultural awareness and understanding in the workplace.

Enhancing Cross-Cultural Communication Skills Effective communication is essential for navigating multicultural settings. This chapter explores strategies for improving cross-cultural communication skills and overcoming language barriers.

The Role of Cultural Intelligence in Leadership Leaders with high CQ can effectively manage diverse teams and drive global success. This section examines how cultural intelligence enhances leadership capabilities and contributes to organizational performance.

6

Chapter 6: Strategies for Multicultural Team Collaboration

B**uilding Trust in Multicultural Teams** Trust is the foundation of effective team collaboration, especially in multicultural settings. This chapter discusses the challenges of building trust in diverse teams and offers strategies for fostering trust and cohesion.

Facilitating Inclusive Meetings and Discussions Inclusive meetings and discussions ensure that all team members have a voice. This section provides practical tips for creating inclusive meeting environments and encouraging diverse perspectives.

Resolving Conflicts in Multicultural Teams Conflicts can arise in any team, but they can be particularly complex in multicultural settings. This chapter explores common sources of conflict in diverse teams and offers strategies for effective conflict resolution.

Leveraging Diverse Perspectives for Innovation Diverse perspectives can drive innovation and creative problem-solving. This section examines how organizations can harness the power of diverse viewpoints to generate new ideas and solutions.

7

Chapter 7: Overcoming Challenges in Diverse Workplaces

Addressing Resistance to Diversity Initiatives Resistance to diversity initiatives can hinder progress and create tension within the organization. This chapter explores common sources of resistance and offers strategies for overcoming them.

Navigating Cultural Differences Cultural differences can lead to misunderstandings and conflicts. This section provides practical tips for navigating cultural differences and promoting harmony in the workplace.

Ensuring Equity and Fairness Equity and fairness are essential for creating an inclusive workplace. This chapter discusses the importance of equitable practices and offers strategies for ensuring fairness in all aspects of the organization.

Sustaining Diversity and Inclusion Efforts Sustaining diversity and inclusion efforts requires ongoing commitment and resources. This section examines how organizations can maintain momentum and continuously improve their diversity initiatives.

8

Chapter 8: The Role of Technology in Promoting Diversity

Advancements in Diversity Technology Technology has the potential to enhance diversity and inclusion efforts. This chapter explores recent advancements in diversity technology and their applications in the workplace.

Leveraging Data Analytics for Diversity Data analytics can provide valuable insights into diversity and inclusion efforts. This section discusses how organizations can use data to measure progress, identify areas for improvement, and inform decision-making.

Implementing AI and Machine Learning for Inclusion Artificial intelligence (AI) and machine learning can help identify and address bias in the workplace. This chapter examines the role of AI in promoting inclusion and offers practical tips for implementation.

The Future of Diversity Technology The future of diversity technology holds exciting possibilities. This section explores emerging trends and technologies that have the potential to further advance diversity and inclusion in the workplace.

9

Chapter 9: The Impact of Diversity on Employee Engagement

Understanding Employee Engagement Employee engagement is critical for organizational success. This chapter introduces the concept of employee engagement and its importance in a diverse workplace.

The Link Between Diversity and Engagement Diversity can positively impact employee engagement by creating a more inclusive and supportive environment. This section explores the connection between diversity and engagement and presents research findings on the topic.

Strategies for Enhancing Engagement in Diverse Workplaces Organizations can implement various strategies to enhance employee engagement in diverse workplaces. This chapter offers practical tips for fostering engagement and creating a positive work environment.

Measuring and Evaluating Engagement Efforts Measuring and evaluating engagement efforts is essential for continuous improvement. This section discusses different methods for assessing engagement and provides guidance on using the results to inform diversity initiatives.

10

Chapter 10: Global Trends in Diversity and Inclusion

Overview of Global Diversity Trends Diversity and inclusion efforts vary across different regions and cultures. This chapter provides an overview of global diversity trends and highlights key differences and similarities.

Regional Approaches to Diversity Different regions have unique approaches to diversity and inclusion. This section examines regional perspectives and practices, offering insights into how organizations can adapt their strategies to different cultural contexts.

International Diversity Initiatives International diversity initiatives can provide valuable lessons and inspiration.

Learning from Global Leaders Studying the practices of organizations that excel in diversity and inclusion can offer valuable insights. This section highlights global leaders in diversity and the innovative strategies they have implemented to create inclusive workplaces.

11

Chapter 11: Measuring the Impact of Diversity Initiatives

Defining Key Performance Indicators (KPIs) for Diversity Establishing clear KPIs for diversity initiatives is essential for measuring success. This chapter discusses how to define and implement KPIs that align with organizational goals and drive meaningful progress.

Collecting and Analyzing Diversity Data Data collection and analysis are crucial for understanding the impact of diversity initiatives. This section explores best practices for gathering and analyzing diversity data to inform decision-making and improve outcomes.

Evaluating the Effectiveness of Diversity Programs Regular evaluation of diversity programs helps organizations identify strengths and areas for improvement. This chapter provides guidance on conducting thorough evaluations and using the findings to enhance diversity efforts.

Reporting and Communicating Results Transparent reporting and communication of diversity outcomes build trust and accountability. This section offers tips for effectively communicating the results of diversity initiatives to stakeholders.

12

Chapter 12: The Future of Work: Embracing Diversity and Innovation

The Changing Nature of Work The future of work is evolving, with increased emphasis on remote work, digital transformation, and flexible arrangements. This chapter explores how these changes impact diversity and inclusion efforts.

Emerging Trends in Diversity and Innovation New trends and technologies continue to shape the landscape of diversity and innovation. This section examines emerging trends and their potential to drive positive change in the workplace.

Preparing for the Future Organizations must proactively prepare for the future by embracing diversity and fostering a culture of innovation. This chapter offers strategies for staying ahead of the curve and ensuring long-term success.

Building a Sustainable and Inclusive Future Sustainability and inclusivity are key components of future success. This section discusses how organizations can integrate these principles into their long-term strategies and create a lasting positive impact.

13

Chapter 13: Case Studies of Successful Multicultural Leadership

Case Study 1: A Global Tech Company's Journey to Inclusion This case study explores how a leading global tech company successfully implemented diversity and inclusion initiatives to enhance innovation and performance.

Case Study 2: A Multinational Corporation's Approach to Cultural Intelligence This chapter examines how a multinational corporation developed cultural intelligence among its leadership team to improve cross-cultural collaboration and drive global success.

Case Study 3: A Healthcare Organization's Commitment to Diversity This case study highlights how a healthcare organization prioritized diversity and inclusion to improve patient care and employee engagement.

Lessons Learned from Case Studies Analyzing these case studies provides valuable lessons and best practices for other organizations looking to enhance their diversity and inclusion efforts.

14

Chapter 14: The Role of Education and Training in Diversity and Innovation

Incorporating Diversity Education in the Workplace Education is a critical component of diversity and inclusion efforts. This chapter explores how organizations can incorporate diversity education into their training programs and foster a culture of continuous learning.

Developing Cultural Competence through Training Cultural competence training helps employees navigate diverse environments and build stronger relationships. This section provides practical tips for developing and implementing effective cultural competence training programs.

Promoting Lifelong Learning and Development Lifelong learning is essential for staying relevant in a rapidly changing world. This chapter discusses how organizations can promote continuous learning and development to support diversity and innovation.

Collaboration with Educational Institutions Partnering with educational institutions can enhance diversity and innovation efforts. This section examines how organizations can collaborate with schools, colleges, and universities to develop a diverse talent pipeline and drive positive change.

15

Chapter 15: Leadership for a Diverse and Innovative Future

The Qualities of Effective Multicultural Leaders Effective multicultural leaders possess unique qualities that enable them to navigate diverse environments and drive innovation. This chapter explores the essential qualities of successful multicultural leaders and how they can be developed.

Building Resilient and Adaptive Leadership Teams Resilience and adaptability are critical for navigating the complexities of a diverse and dynamic world. This section discusses strategies for building resilient and adaptive leadership teams that can thrive in the face of change.

Fostering a Culture of Innovation and Inclusion Creating a culture that embraces both innovation and inclusion is key to long-term success. This chapter offers practical tips for fostering a culture where creativity and diversity are valued and celebrated.

Leading the Way to a Better Future The future of business depends on leaders who can harness the power of diversity and drive global innovation. This concluding section inspires leaders to take bold actions and lead the way to a more inclusive and innovative future.

Book Description: Synergy in Diversity: Elevating Business Through Multicultural Leadership and Global Innovation

In an increasingly interconnected world, the power of diversity is no longer a mere buzzword but a strategic imperative. *Synergy in Diversity* delves into the transformative potential of multicultural leadership and global innovation to revolutionize modern businesses. This thought-provoking book offers a comprehensive guide to harnessing the unique strengths of a diverse workforce to drive creativity, collaboration, and competitive advantage.

Through fifteen insightful chapters, readers will explore the evolution of diversity in the workplace, the critical role of inclusive leadership, and practical strategies for building multicultural teams. The book highlights the significance of cultural intelligence, the impact of technology on diversity efforts, and the undeniable link between diversity and employee engagement. With a keen focus on real-world applications, *Synergy in Diversity* presents case studies of successful organizations that have embraced diversity to fuel their innovation engines and achieve remarkable business outcomes.

Whether you're a business leader, HR professional, or simply passionate about fostering an inclusive workplace, this book offers valuable insights and actionable strategies to elevate your organization. *Synergy in Diversity* is your essential companion on the journey to creating a vibrant, innovative, and globally competitive business.

www.ingramcontent.com/pod-product-compliance
Lightning Source LLC
LaVergne TN
LVHW020509080526
838202LV00057B/6261